The Official

CHOCOLATE CANDIES

History of

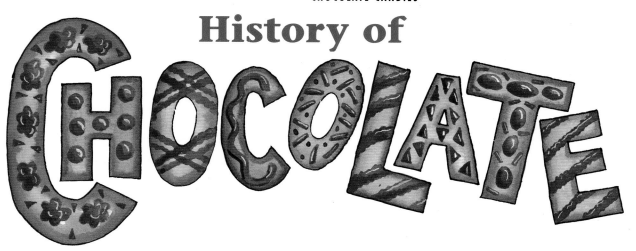

by Red, Yellow, Green, and Blue

Illustrated by Karen E. Pellaton

Charlesbridge

To everyone who is sweet and delightful

To Papa, who loves chocolate
–K. E. P.

To Red. Red is the best.

Published by Charlesbridge Publishing
85 Main Street
Watertown, MA 02472
(617) 926-0329
www.charlesbridge.com

Printed in South Korea
(hc) 10 9 8 7 6 5 4 3 2 1
(sc) 10 9 8 7 6 5 4 3 2 1

Library of Congress Cataloging-in-Publication Data
The official "M&M's"® Brand history of chocolate /
by Red, Yellow, Green, and Blue!; illustrated by
Karen E. Pellaton.
    p.   cm.
Includes bibliographical references.
ISBN 1-57091-448-6 (reinforced for library use)
ISBN 1-57091-449-4 (softcover)
1. Chocolate—Juvenile literature. (1. Chocolate.)
I. Title: Official M&M's brand book of chocolate.
II. Title: Official M and M's brand book of chocolate.
III. Pellaton, Karen E., ill.
TX415.033   2001
641.3'374—dc21   00-063889

The illustrations in this book were done in watercolor
    on Arches watercolor paper.
The display type and text type were set in Futura,
    Stone Informal, and Stone Sans.
Color separations were made by Sung In Printing, Inc.,
    South Korea.
Printed and bound by Sung In Printing, Inc., South Korea
Production supervision by Brian G. Walker
Designed by Diane M. Earley

CHOCOLATE.

Sweet, smooth, yummy chocolate. Almost everybody loves it, and some can't get enough of it. People use chocolate to celebrate a special occasion, to comfort a friend, or simply to treat themselves to something special. We serve it frozen, liquid, and in every shape imaginable. So how did chocolate get so popular?

Chocolate? How 'bout a book on peanuts?

No! Chocolate is much more important.

Americans eat three billion pounds of chocolate each year! That would be enough "M&M's"® Chocolate Candies to reach to the moon and back . . . eleven times!

The mighty Amazon and Orinoco Rivers in South America flow past giant trees with chocolate trunks and chocolate-chip leaves. . . .

Yeah, right! There's no such thing as a chocolate tree!

Actually, smart guy, there is. Only it's not made of chocolate; it GROWS chocolate!

The chocolate tree is called the cacao (ka-KOW). It's a beautiful flowering tree that grew wild in South and Central America more than four thousand years ago. Today, people have planted cacao in warm, rainy places all over the world.

Tropic of Cancer

Equator

Tropic of Capricorn

Cacao grows near the equator where the temperature stays about eighty degrees Fahrenheit, and the air is always full of moisture. The best home for a cacao tree is a tropical rainforest.

Some historians believe the word *cacao* comes from the Aztec word *cacahuatl* (ka-ka-HWA-til), but others trace it back to the Maya name for cocoa, kakaw (ka-KOW), which was written like this:

This isn't my idea of a tropical paradise. There are too many bugs! They're so annoying.

I know what you mean. I can think of another pest I'd like to get rid of.

A wild cacao tree can grow fifty feet tall, with leaves up to one foot long. Because it needs so much moisture, cacao grows best in the shade of an even taller tree. The shade protects the young cacao plant from the hot, dry rays of the sun. Flies and tiny insects called midges also flourish in a damp environment. That's important for chocolate because these insects pollinate the cacao trees. Without flies and midges, no new trees would grow.

Cacao flowers grow right out of the tree trunk and eventually turn into fruits that look like small, football-shaped bean pods. A single tree might have both flowers and pods at the same time. Each pod holds between twenty-five and fifty inch-long beans surrounded by sweet, sticky, white pulp.

Monkeys, squirrels, and other animals like to eat cacao pulp, but the beans taste too bitter. Because the beans are really the tree's seeds, the animals help plant more cacao trees when they spit the beans out onto the ground.

When the pods are ripe, cacao growers cut them off the tree one at a time using a long blade on the end of a pole. A full-grown tree might yield about fifty pods. That's enough to make about seven pounds of chocolate.

The cacao tree belongs to the same family as the kola tree, which gives us the flavor for cola drinks.

The cutter must be careful not to damage the flowers, trunk, or any unripe pods. Bruised or cut parts of the tree easily become diseased, so the work is done carefully by hand, not by machines.

Workers then split open the pods and remove the beans and pulp, which they pile between banana leaves or in wooden crates and lay in the hot sun to ferment. This process is called curing, and it helps to develop the natural chocolate flavor of the beans. Heat from the sun makes them turn brown. The pulp changes into a liquid and drains away.

After the beans are fully cured, they have to dry under direct sunlight for about a week so that they won't grow mold. Finally, workers scoop the dried beans into big bags weighing up to two hundred pounds and send them to chocolate factories all over the world.

There are three main types of cacao, and each has a slightly different taste. Criollo trees are easily damaged, so their beans are rare, but most people think they have the best aroma and flavor. Forastero trees are hardier, and their beans make up ninety percent of the world's crop. A hybrid tree, called the trinitario, combines the best qualities of both varieties—great aroma and great strength. Most chocolate is made from blending different amounts of all three kinds of beans.

Wait, you're jumping ahead. Who invented chocolate anyhow?

People have been harvesting cacao in much the same way for thousands of years. Nobody knows who first learned to grow it, but it was already an important part of the life of the Maya people in Central Mexico way back in the third century. They used the beans to make different hot and cold drinks and powders for food, medicine, and religious ceremonies. Cacao beans were so valuable then, they were even used as money!

250-800
The Maya civilization reaches the peak of its development. The Maya cultivate cacao and decorate special pots used only for chocolate drinks.

Who says money doesn't grow on trees?

Cacao beans were an established currency in Central America right up until the late 1800s. Before Columbus landed in the New World, you could buy a rabbit for about eight beans. After Spain took control of Central America, many people paid their taxes with cacao beans.

In the fourteeth century, the Aztec empire spread throughout Central Mexico. The Aztecs believed that the first cacao was brought from heaven by a god named Quetzalcoatl (Kets-ahl-ko-AH-til). Scientists later based the scientific name for the tree on this belief. They named it *Theobroma cacao*, which means "chocolate food of the gods."

Another reason to worship me.

Not quite, buddy.

Like other civilizations before them, the Aztecs used cacao beans to make a special drink, which they called cacahuatl (ka-ka-HWA-til). This wasn't anything like the chocolate drinks we enjoy today.

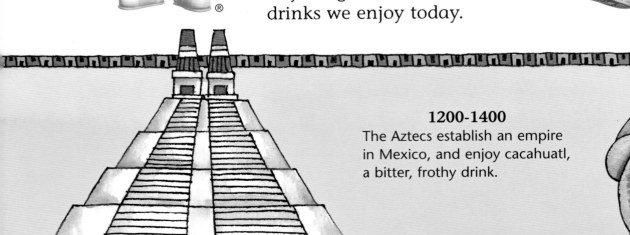

1200-1400
The Aztecs establish an empire in Mexico, and enjoy cacahuatl, a bitter, frothy drink.

The Aztecs mixed ground-up cacao beans with powdered chilies, cornmeal, and spices. Then they added water and poured the concoction from one jug to another until it was very frothy. They may have also used a wooden swizzle stick to make the froth. The result was a thick, peppery sludge, but people seemed to like it. One Aztec king, Montezuma II, is said to have drunk up to fifty cups a day!

Peppery sludge? Yuck!

In the hot summer months, Montezuma II would send servants to the mountains near his capital city, Tenochtitlán, to bring back snow and ice, which he then mixed with cacahuatl. He may have been the first person ever to enjoy a frozen chocolate treat!

1502
Columbus discovers cacao beans on his fourth voyage. He doesn't see any value in them.

1502-1520
Montezuma II reigns as emperor of the Aztecs. He holds grand banquets at which cacahuatl is served.

It was as a cold, bitter drink that Spanish explorer Hernán Cortés first tasted chocolate in 1519. Cortés didn't like it, but he saw how valuable cacao was in the New World, so he brought back the beans and the recipe for making cacahuatl when he returned to Spain.

1519
Hernán Cortés encounters the Aztecs and tastes chocolate for the first time.

1585
The first official shipment of cacao beans is sent to Spain. The Spanish add sugar and honey to make chocolate sweet.

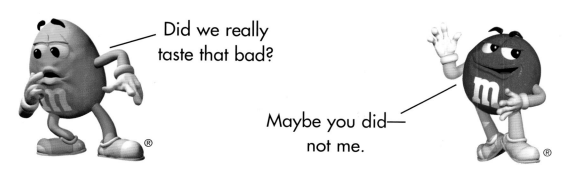

Did we really taste that bad?

Maybe you did—not me.

At first, the recipe for chocolate was top secret. Only the Spanish nobility could enjoy the drink. They liked it better sweetened, so they added sugar, honey, and even orange or rose water. Then someone decided to try it hot instead of cold, and sweet hot chocolate was born!

But Spain couldn't keep chocolate a secret for long. Already, travelers were taking an interest in the new drink. When a Spanish princess married a French prince in 1615, the secret got out, and all of Europe quickly became crazy for chocolate.

Finally! The fame I deserve.

1615
Princess Anne of Spain marries Louis XIII of France, taking the recipe for chocolate with her.

Royal Chocolate Recipe

1657
A shopkeeper from Paris travels to London and opens England's first chocolate shop.

By 1700, chocolate drink shops were fashionable places to meet all over Europe. People would sip chocolate and debate the issues of the day. Pretty soon, chocolate drinks were so popular that factories started to produce them. More chocolate meant cheaper chocolate, and soon more and more people could afford to drink it.

1662
An English doctor prescribes chocolate as a medicine.

1712
A Boston drugstore advertises chocolate for sale.

1728
The first chocolate factory in the world opens in Bristol, England.

It was around this time that someone in France or England thought of drinking chocolate in milk instead of water. They also tried adding eggs, starch, and even brick dust, but it was chocolate milk that really captured the world's taste buds.

1755
Massachusetts sea captains begin to trade directly with Caribbean farms for cacao beans.

1765
The first chocolate factory in colonial America opens in Massachusetts.

For all the experimentation, chocolate was still a thick, greasy drink at the beginning of the nineteenth century. A real breakthrough came in 1828 when a Dutch chemist patented a press to squeeze out almost all of the oily cocoa butter from the crushed beans. For the first time, people could make a cup of hot chocolate with the dry, fine powder we see in stores today.

What could be done with all the rich, yummy, leftover cocoa butter? Those solid slabs gave one British chocolate maker an idea: He added extra cocoa butter to the chocolate powder and made the world's first chocolate bars in 1847!

Hey, you gotta start somewhere.

The world's most famous chocolate cake was invented in 1832 by a sixteen-year-old boy in Austria. Franz Sacher combined rich chocolate batter with an apricot-jam glaze and smooth chocolate frosting. He called it the Sachertorte, and it was known for more than a century as the best chocolate cake in the world.

1828
A Dutch chemist invents a hand-operated cocoa press that separates cocoa butter from cocoa solids.

1832
A sixteen-year-old boy invents what will become the world's most famous chocolate cake—the Sachertorte.

1847
The first-ever chocolate bars are produced in England.

White chocolate is a combination of cocoa butter, milk, and sugar. No actual chocolate goes into the mix! Today leftover cocoa butter is also used in suntan lotion, shaving cream, paint, soap, and some salad dressings.

Another big breakthrough came in 1876 in Switzerland. Two men experimenting with condensed milk tried combining it with the new hard chocolate. Sweet, solid milk chocolate quickly became a favorite treat all over the world.

1860
The first chocolate candy shop in the United States opens for business.

1876
Solid milk chocolate gives Switzerland a delicious new treat.

Over in the American colonies, people were watching the development of chocolate with eager, hungry eyes. By 1755, Massachusetts sea captains had begun to trade for cacao beans directly with farms in the Caribbean instead of importing the beans from Europe. By 1765, the first chocolate drink factory had been built, and almost one hundred years later, the first chocolate candy shop had opened. By 1885, chocolate had become so popular that a California chocolate maker was importing two hundred tons of cacao beans every year!

During World War I, the American army sent slabs of chocolate to troops serving overseas. When the war ended and the soldiers came home, they didn't want to give up their sweet, yummy treats. More and more chocolate companies sprang up to meet the demand, turning out all kinds of drops, bars, chips, and filled and coated candies. America was dipped in chocolate, and everybody loved it.

Yeah, OK, but let's get to me!

1911
Candy bars (bars of chocolate mixed with other sweets) are sold in the United States for the first time.

1914
Chocolate bars are issued as emergency rations for American army troops during World War I.

Americans were soon eating several pounds of chocolate every year, but sales dropped sharply in the hot summer months because chocolate melted too easily. In 1941, colorful candy coatings that could withstand the summer heat solved the problem. "M&M's"® Chocolate Candies were an immediate success, satisfying America's sweet tooth all year long.

That's better. But you forgot to mention which of us is everyone's favorite color.

Isn't it Blue?

The "M&M's"® family:
1941 Plain
1954 Peanut
1988 Almond
1989 Mint
1990 Peanut butter
1996 "M&M's"® MINIs and COLORWORKS®
1998 Crispy

1934
Captain Paul Logan creates a chocolate energy bar for military troops called "Ration D," but it doesn't taste as good as the chocolate Americans have become accustomed to.

1941
"M&M's"® Plain Chocolate Candies make their debut! American soldiers serving in World War II enjoyed the yummy chocolate that didn't melt in the heat.

Um, maybe we should go.
I'm getting nervous.

Please! Who'd
want to eat you?

Some people eat chocolate for more than just a tasty snack. In the sixteenth century, Europeans thought a chocolate drink was as nutritious as a full meal. In the seventeenth century, doctors prescribed chocolate drinks as medicine for indigestion, headaches, and general ill health. Today science is finding that a little bit of chocolate can be good for you! Chocolate contains protein and carbohydrates, which give you energy, as well as vitamins, minerals, and antioxidants, which help keep your body healthy.

1950
The letter "M"® is printed on each "M&M's"® Chocolate Candies piece for the first time.

1954
The "M&M's"® Characters are born!

Hello!

I say you've either got it, or you don't.

All the good stuff packed into a small amount of chocolate makes it an ideal food to carry as an emergency ration. Way back in 1519, Cortés noticed that Aztec soldiers who were given chocolate to drink seemed to be able to march for days. More than two centuries later, British sailors and soldiers were given chocolate as part of their rations to help keep up their strength—and their morale.

The U.S. government sent chocolate to soldiers in the Philippines in 1898, and it became a staple for American soldiers during World War I and World War II. In 1984, astronauts on the space shuttle *Columbia* even brought "M&M's"® Chocolate Candies into space, proving that chocolate is truly out of this world!

The trick has always been to convince soldiers and explorers throughout history to save their chocolate for an emergency. Most just can't wait to enjoy the yummy chocolate treat.

1984
"M&M's"® Chocolate Candies blast into space on the shuttle *Columbia*.

2000
"M&M's"® Chocolate Candies become "The Official Candy of the New Millennium."™

Don't we look great now?

So, uh, do they still crush all those beans by hand?

Pay attention, will ya?

Today, chocolate makers use machinery to help them produce enough chocolate to satisfy the world's sweet tooth. When the cacao beans arrive at the chocolate factory from the farm, inspectors check them carefully for quality and sort them by variety before placing them in a roaster. Each kind of bean roasts at a different temperature and for a different length of time to develop the best possible flavor.

INSPECTING

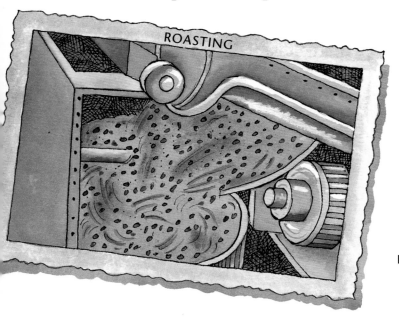

ROASTING

I love a midday sauna.

SHELLING

After roasting, the beans move to a machine called a winnower, which cracks open their outer cases. A blast of air blows away the shells, and the kernels, known as nibs, move on to the mixer.

Giant rollers inside the mixer grind the nibs into a thick, shiny, brown liquid called cocoa liquor. This is the basic ingredient in most chocolate foods.

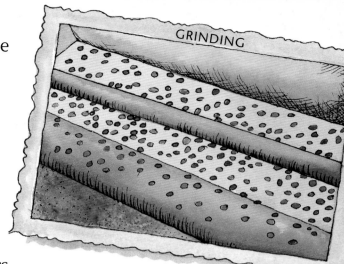

GRINDING

PRESSING

Chocolate makers use the chocolate liquid in lots of different ways. To make cocoa, they pour it into a big press that heats and squeezes the chocolate until almost all its cocoa butter drains out into a basin. What's left is a grainy, hard disk of cocoa. Another machine then grinds the disk into cocoa powder for hot chocolate and chocolate milk and for baking yummy chocolate foods like cookies and cupcakes.

To make chocolate bars, the factory workers pour the chocolate liquid into a big mixer. Then they add sugar and some of the cocoa butter they collected when they made cocoa. If the chocolate makers want to make milk chocolate bars, they add milk to the recipe. Otherwise, the chocolate will be rich and dark.

This is getting confusing!

Ingredients in Chocolate

KEY	BITTER BAKING CHOCOLATE	SEMI SWEET CHOCOLATE	SWEET CHOCOLATE	MILK CHOCOLATE	WHITE CHOCOLATE
MILK	ABOUT 5%	ABOUT 50%	ABOUT 70%	ABOUT 20%	ABOUT 25%
SUGAR	ABOUT 95%			ABOUT 50%	ABOUT 55%
ADDED COCOA BUTTER		ABOUT 15%	ABOUT 15%	ABOUT 20%	
CACAO BEANS GROUND INTO LIQUID		ABOUT 35%	ABOUT 15%	ABOUT 10%	ABOUT 20%

After the mixer combines all the right ingredients, the chocolate flows into a machine called a conche. Heavy rollers blend the chocolate for several hours to make it extra smooth and creamy.

CONCHING

TEMPERING

Still another machine alternately heats and cools the conched chocolate until all the cocoa butter crystals are the same size. This is called tempering, and it's what makes chocolate bars shine and snap when you break them.

People always say I'm a snappy dresser.

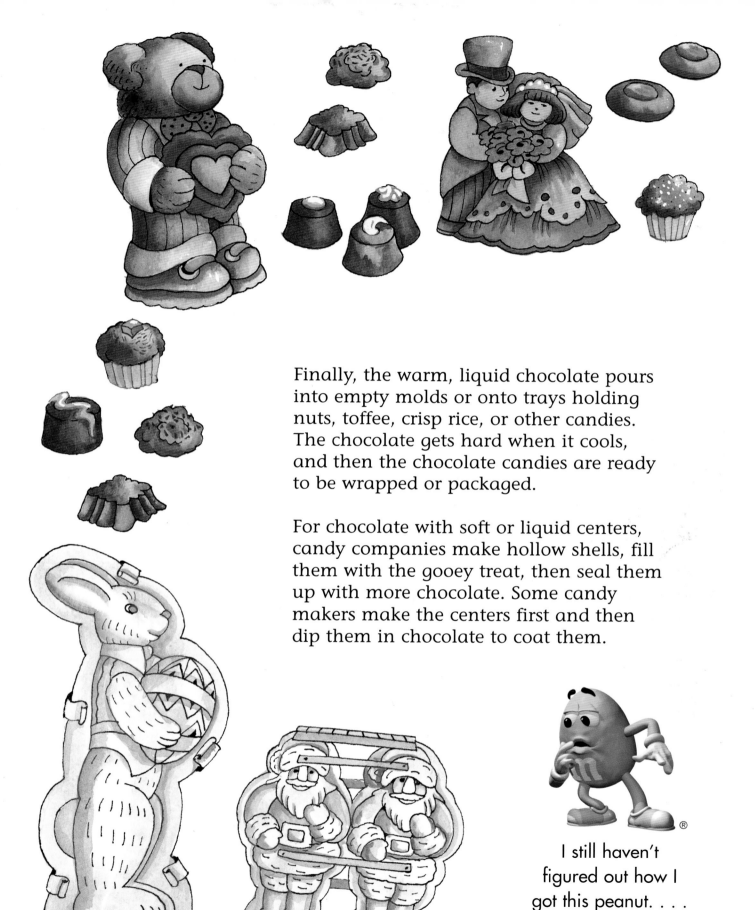

Finally, the warm, liquid chocolate pours into empty molds or onto trays holding nuts, toffee, crisp rice, or other candies. The chocolate gets hard when it cools, and then the chocolate candies are ready to be wrapped or packaged.

For chocolate with soft or liquid centers, candy companies make hollow shells, fill them with the gooey treat, then seal them up with more chocolate. Some candy makers make the centers first and then dip them in chocolate to coat them.

I still haven't figured out how I got this peanut. . . .

"M&M's"® Chocolate Candies are made in a special way. After a machine makes the milk chocolate centers, another machine tumbles them around until they are smooth and rounded. Next, a big drumlike container sprays them all over with a colorful candy shell. When the coating is dry, the candies fall onto movable plates that pass under the special machine that stamps the letter "m"® onto each chocolate candy. Some people say it stands for the sound of a person eating chocolate: "Mmmmmmmm. . . ."

Mmmmmmmm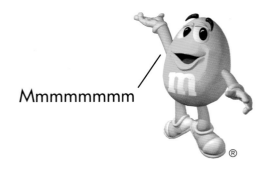

I still think I'm the only one who deserves an "m."®

Chocolate has come a long way from its start as a bitter bean that made a peppery drink. The journey from cacao to cocoa and cacahuatl to chocolate is one of exciting exploration, amazing inventions, and yummy discoveries. People today can enjoy chocolate at any time of the day, all year round. Try a warm cup of cocoa with your breakfast on a cold winter morning. Enjoy a chocolate ice-cream treat on a hot summer afternoon. Linger over a slice of chocolate cake with chocolate frosting after supper to celebrate a birthday—it doesn't matter whose! Whenever you taste that heavenly flavor, you're helping to write the history of chocolate.

Chocolate isn't only for dessert. In the eighteenth century, cookbooks in Italy suggested lasagna spiced with chocolate, chocolate soup, and even chocolate-dipped liver. Many Mexican dishes today are served with mole, an unsweetened, spicy sauce made with chocolate.

For further reading about chocolate:

Ammon, Richard. *The Kid's Book of Chocolate*. New York, NY: Atheneum, 1987.

Busenberg, Bonnie. *Vanilla, Chocolate, and Strawberry: The Story of Your Favorite Flavors*. Minneapolis, MN: Lerner Publications, 1994.

Dineen, Jacqueline. *Chocolate*. Minneapolis, MN: Carolrhoda Books, 1991.

Woods, Samuel G. *Chocolate from Start to Finish*. Woodbridge, CT: Blackbirch Press, 1999.

Find out about chocolate on the Internet:

Cocoapro™ Mars, Incorporated

Learn more about history, nutritional value, and manufacturing of chocolate.
www.cocoapro.com

The Chocolate Manufacturers' Association

Find out about chocolate from tree to finished candy and learn how we all came to know and love this sweet treat.
www.candyusa.org/chocstry.html

Kid's Candy!

A whole site devoted to candy and kids, with trivia, nutritional information, recipes, contests, and more!
www.kidscandy.org

"M&M's" Network™

See Red, Yellow, Green, and Blue at work!
www.m-ms.com

The Sweet Lure of Chocolate

Discover the history of chocolate, join a virtual tour of a chocolate factory, and find out why eating chocolate makes us feel so good.
www.exploratorium.edu/exploring/ exploring_chocolate